THIS COLORING BOOK
BELONGS TO:

....

....

....

ENJOY!

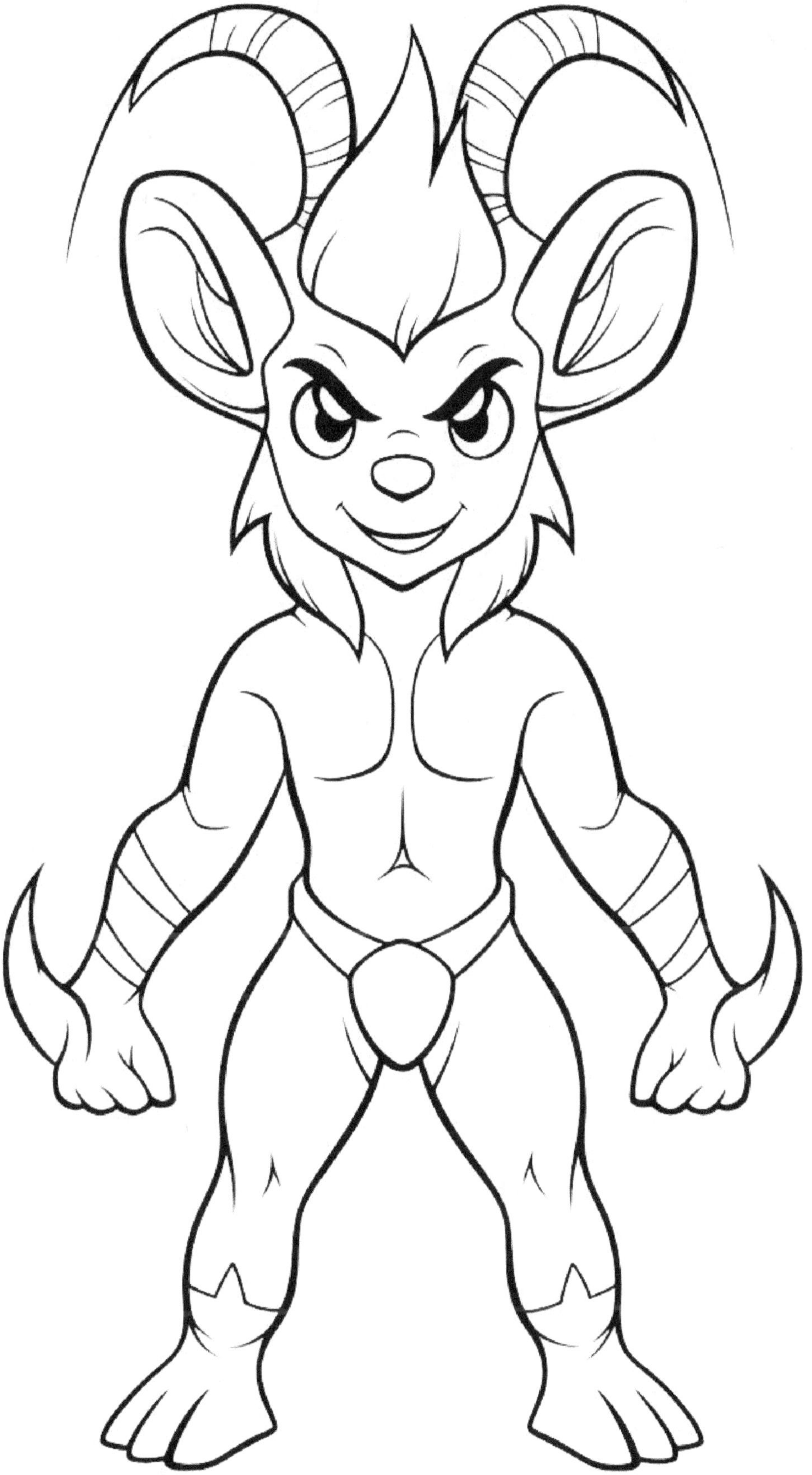

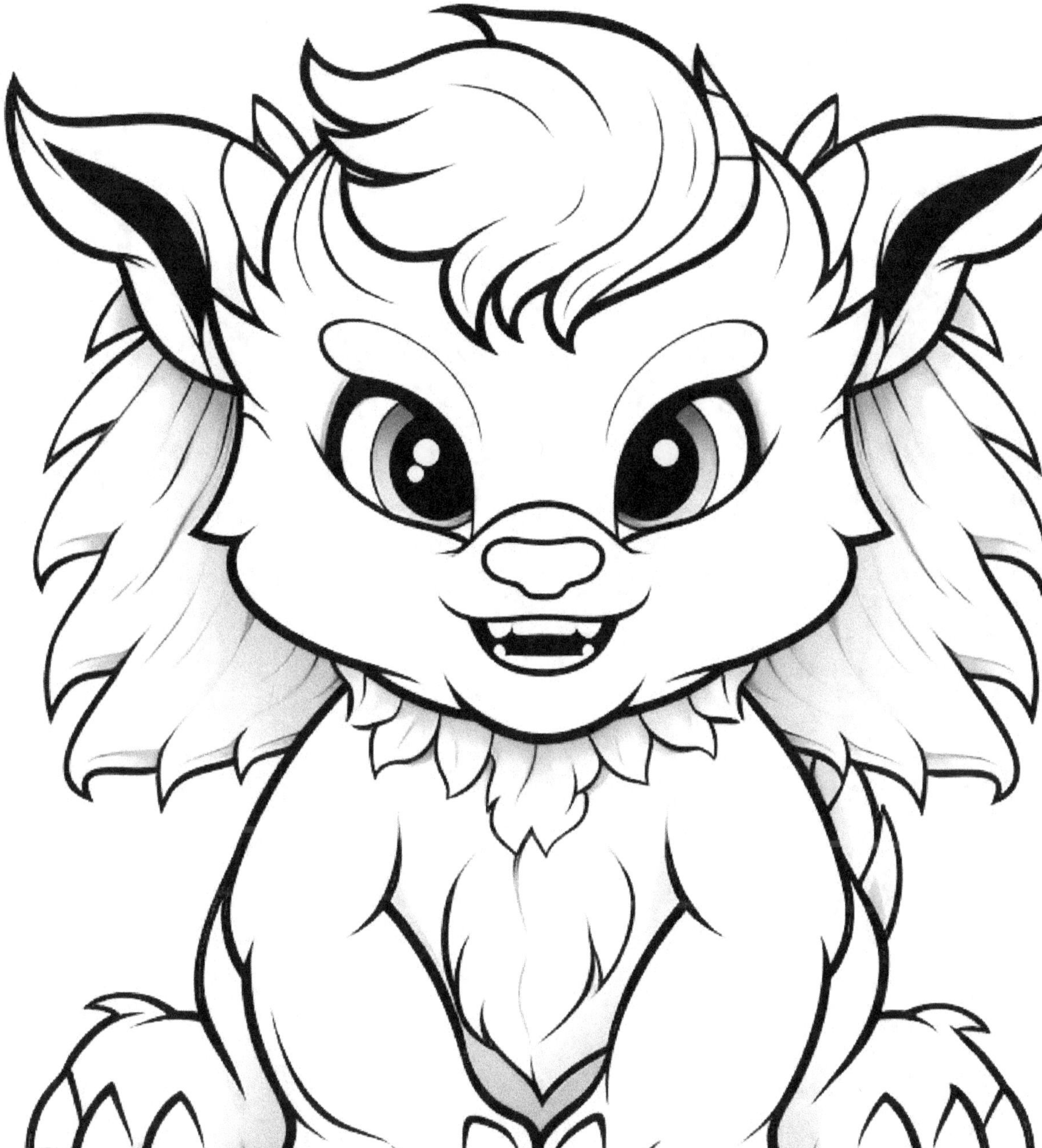

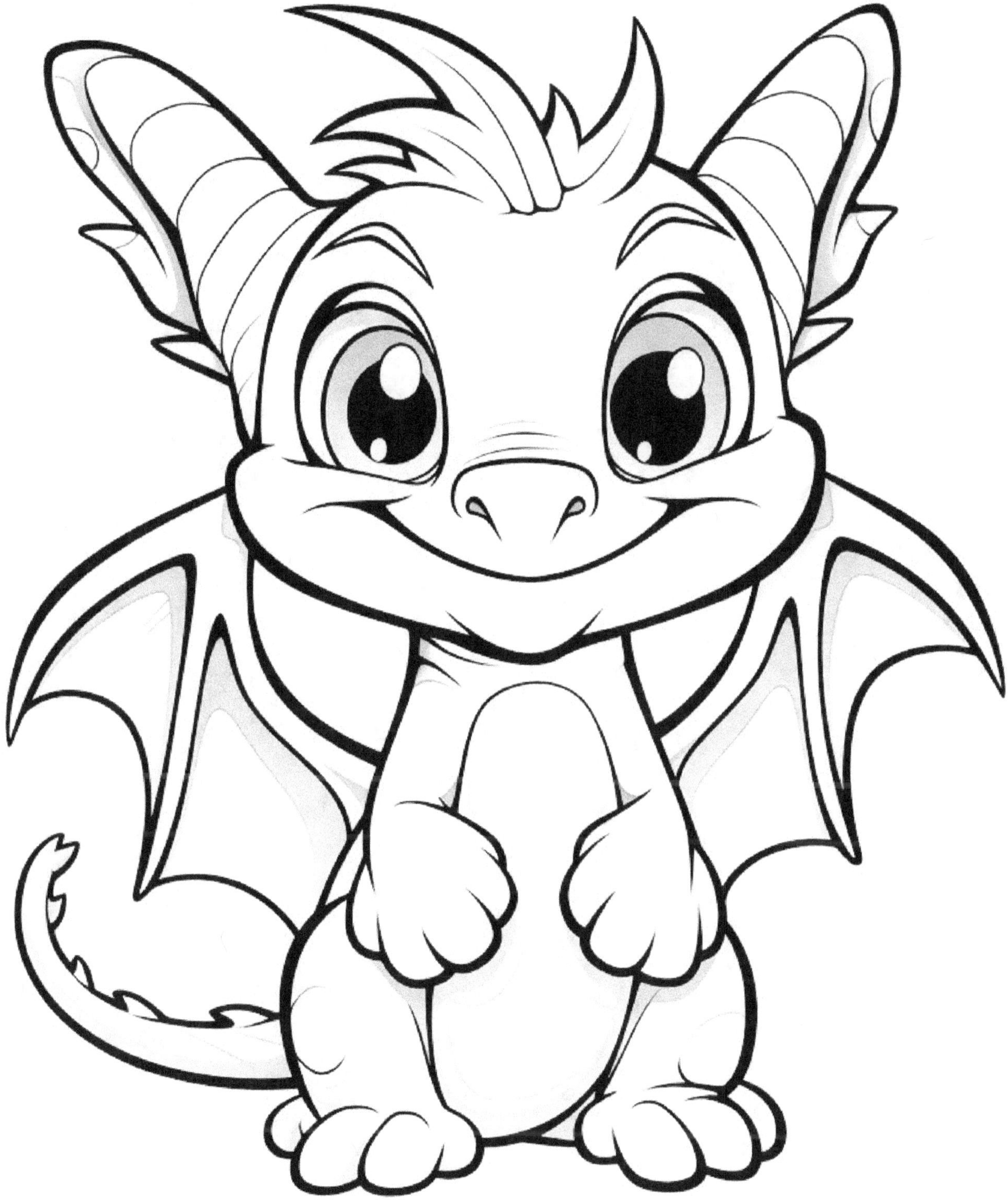

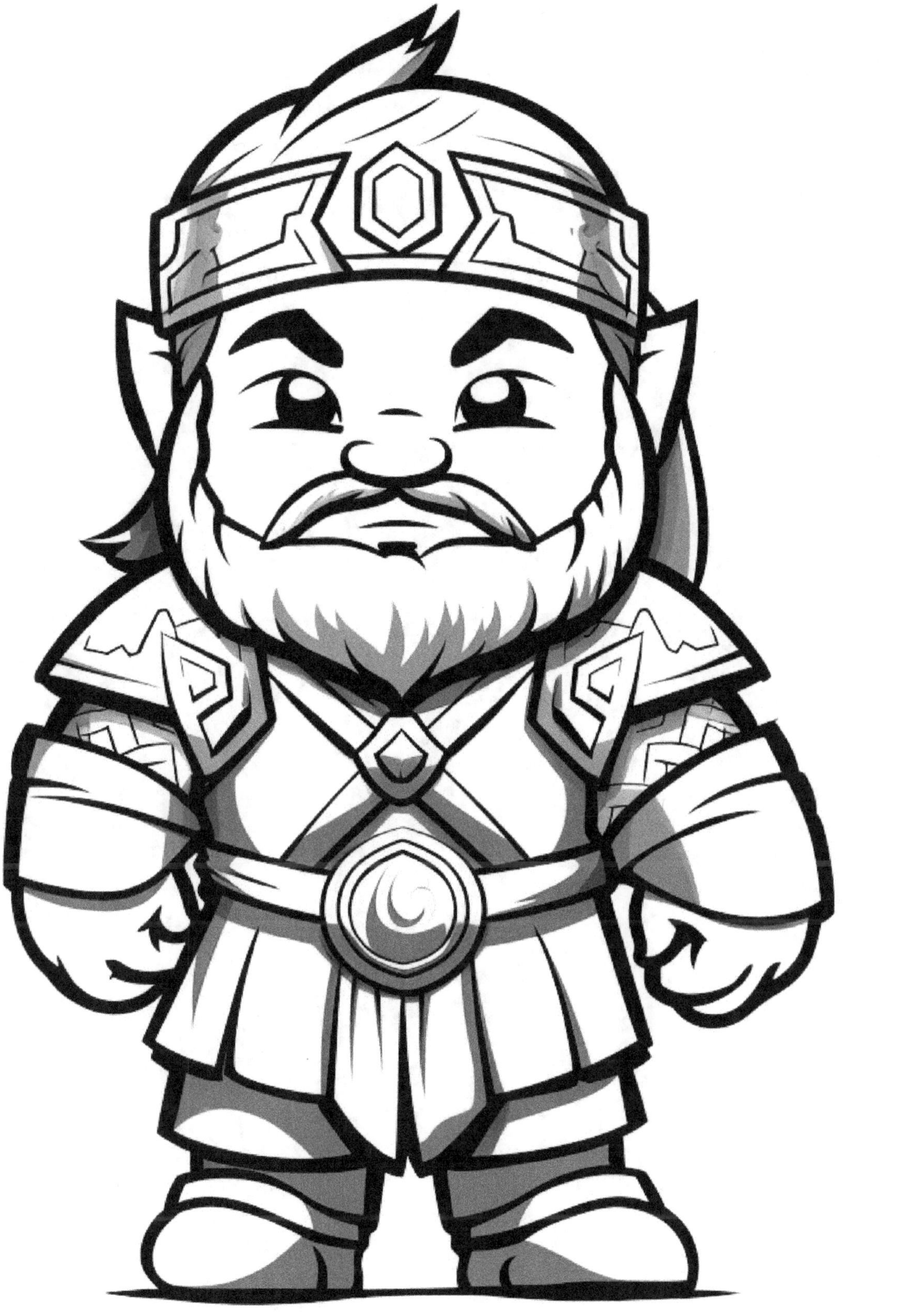

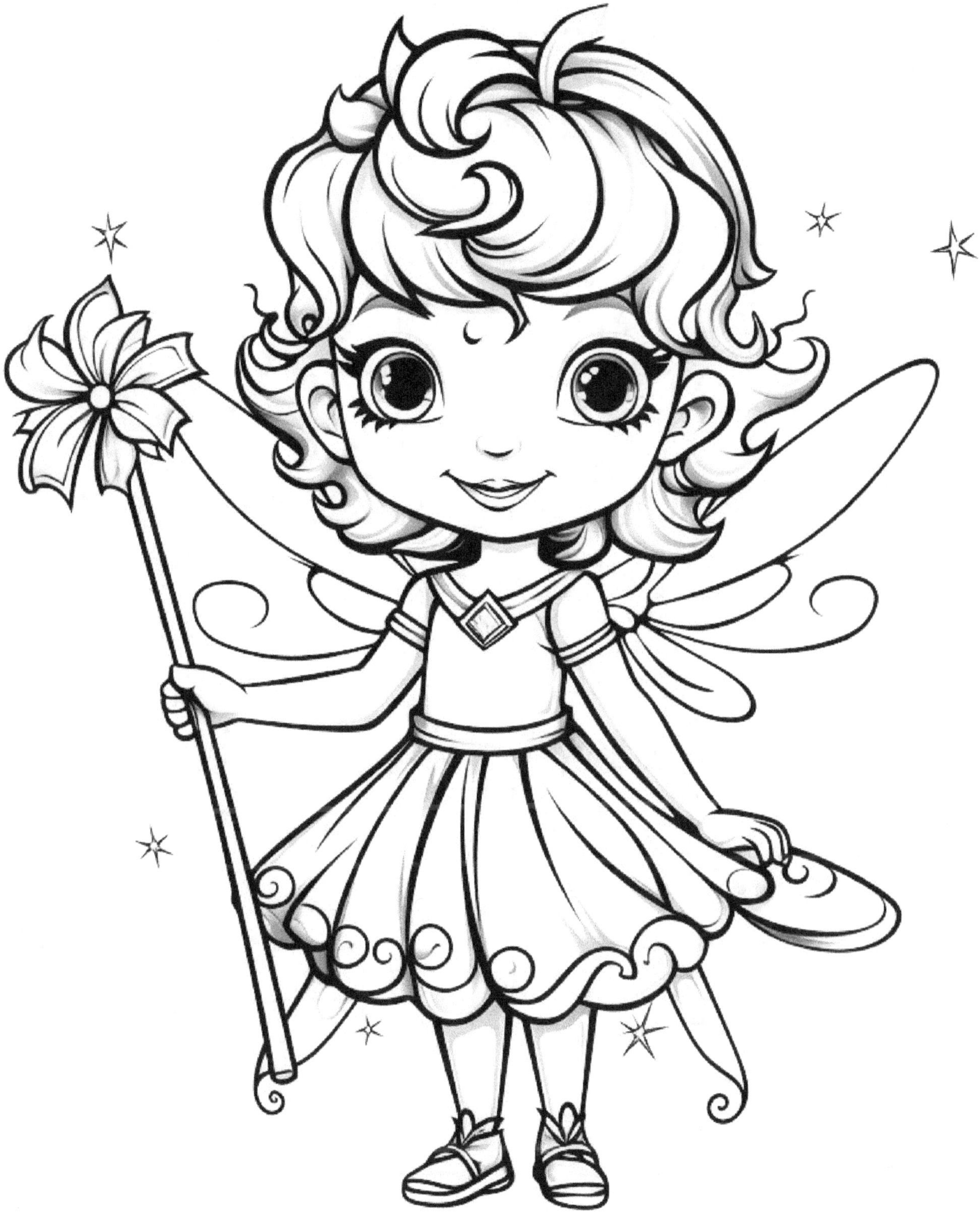

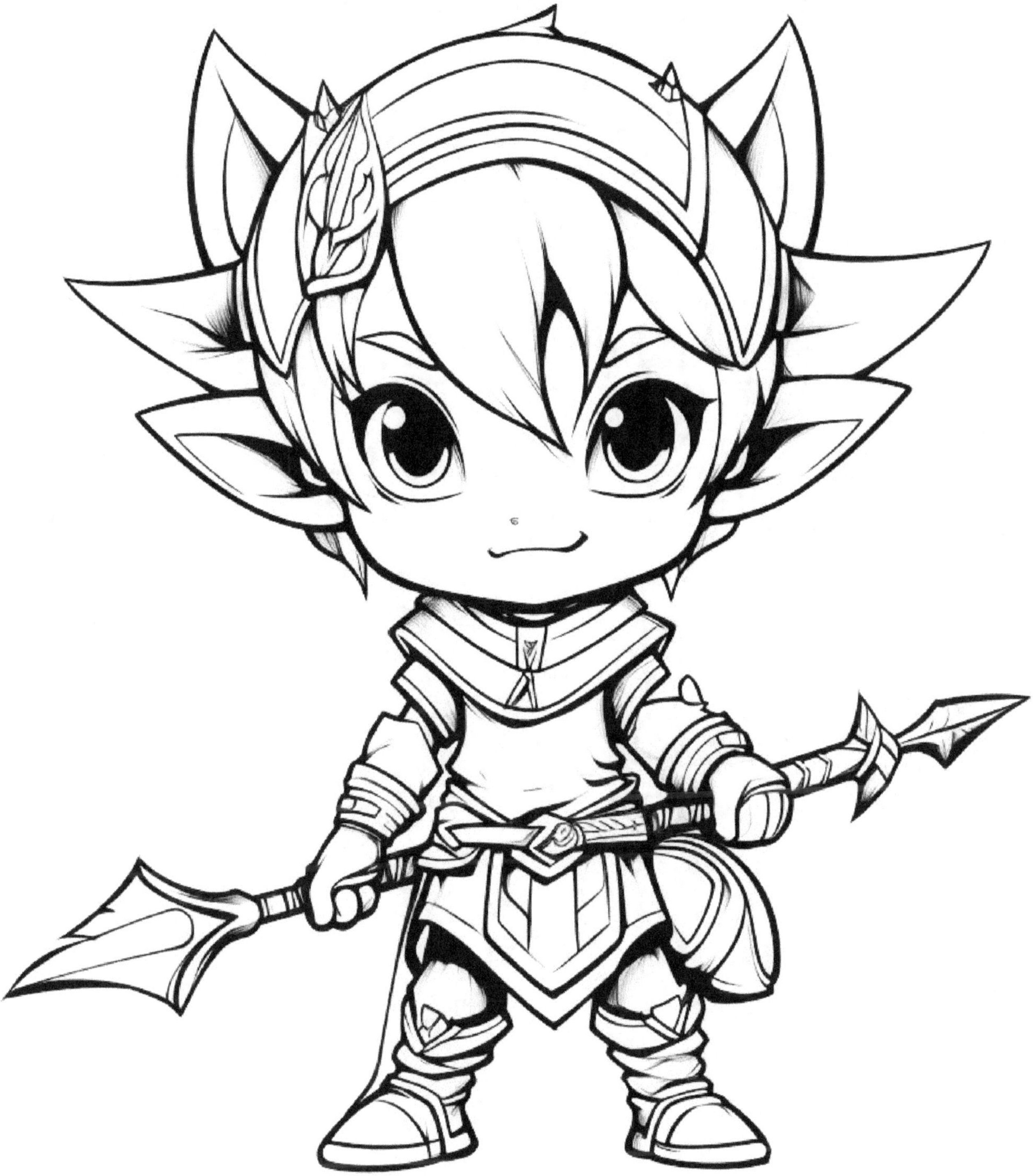

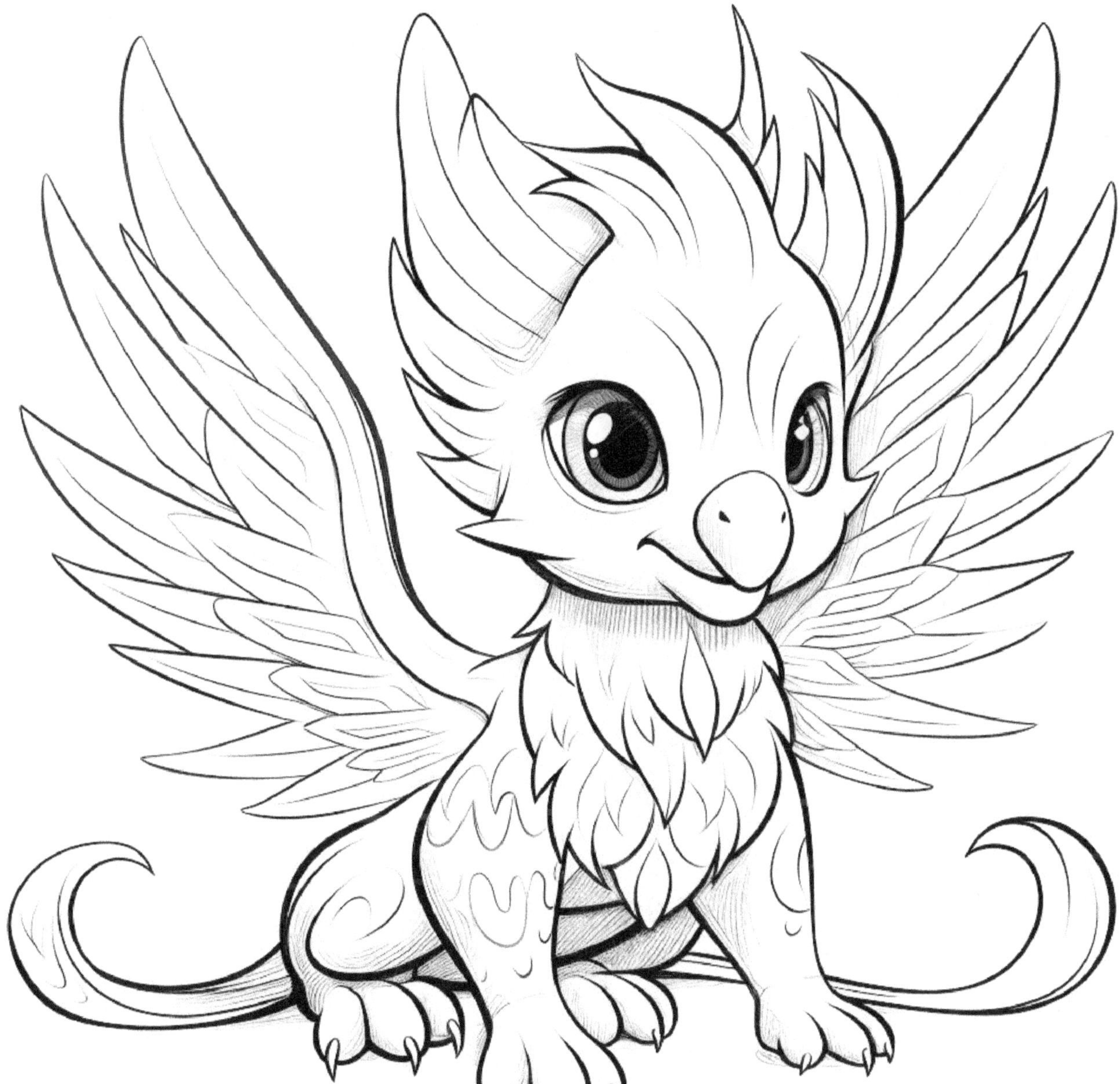

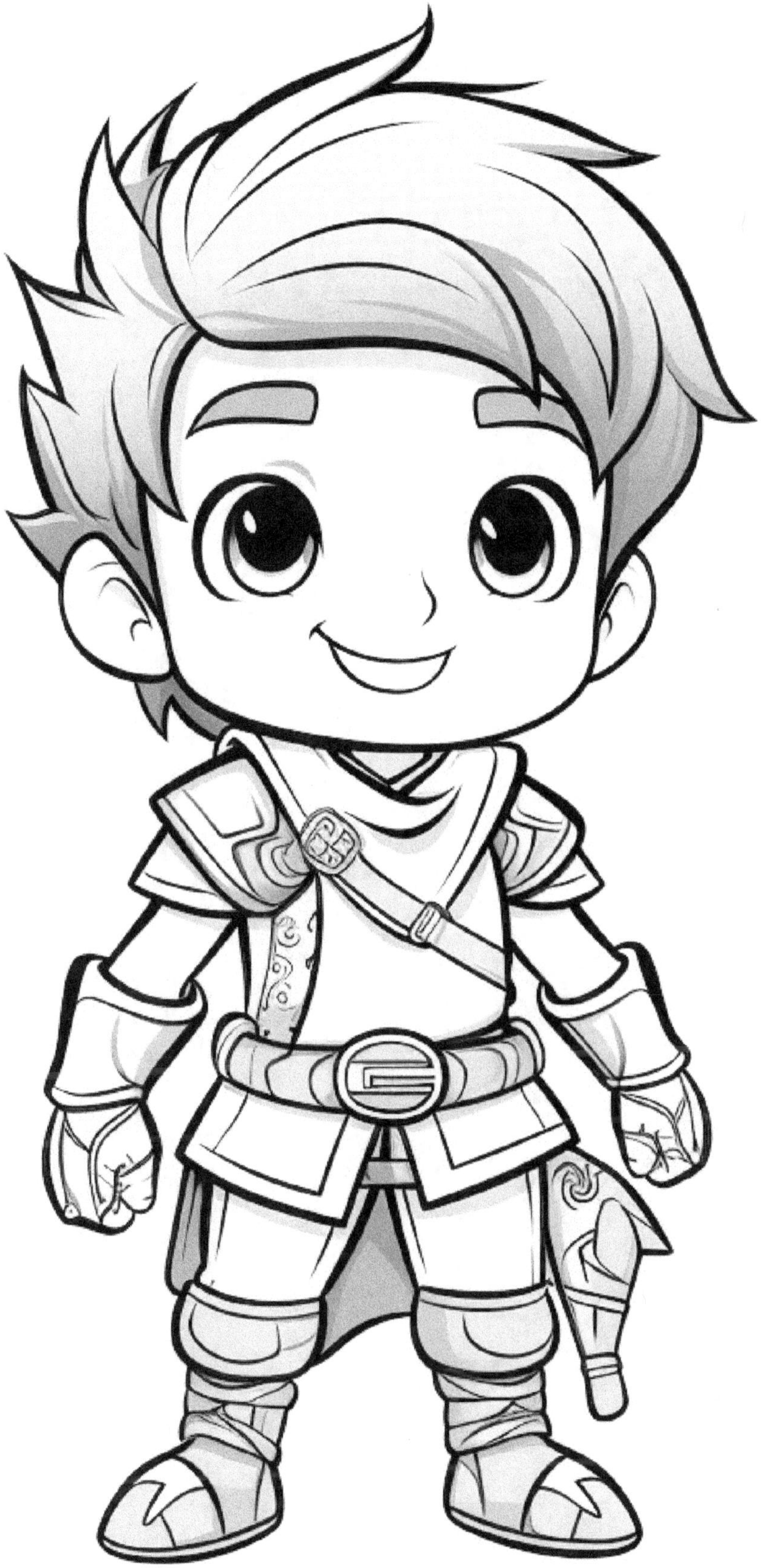

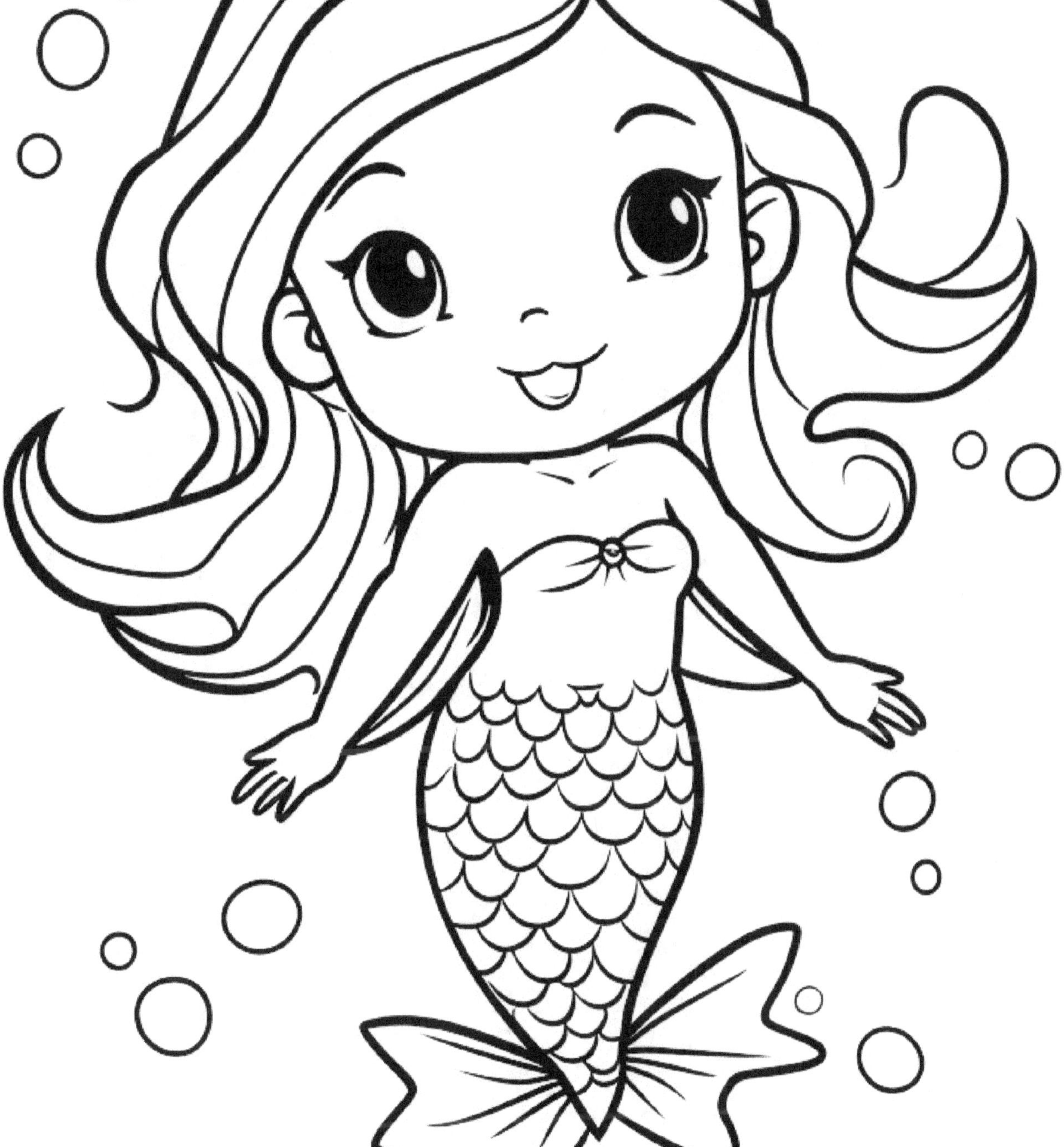

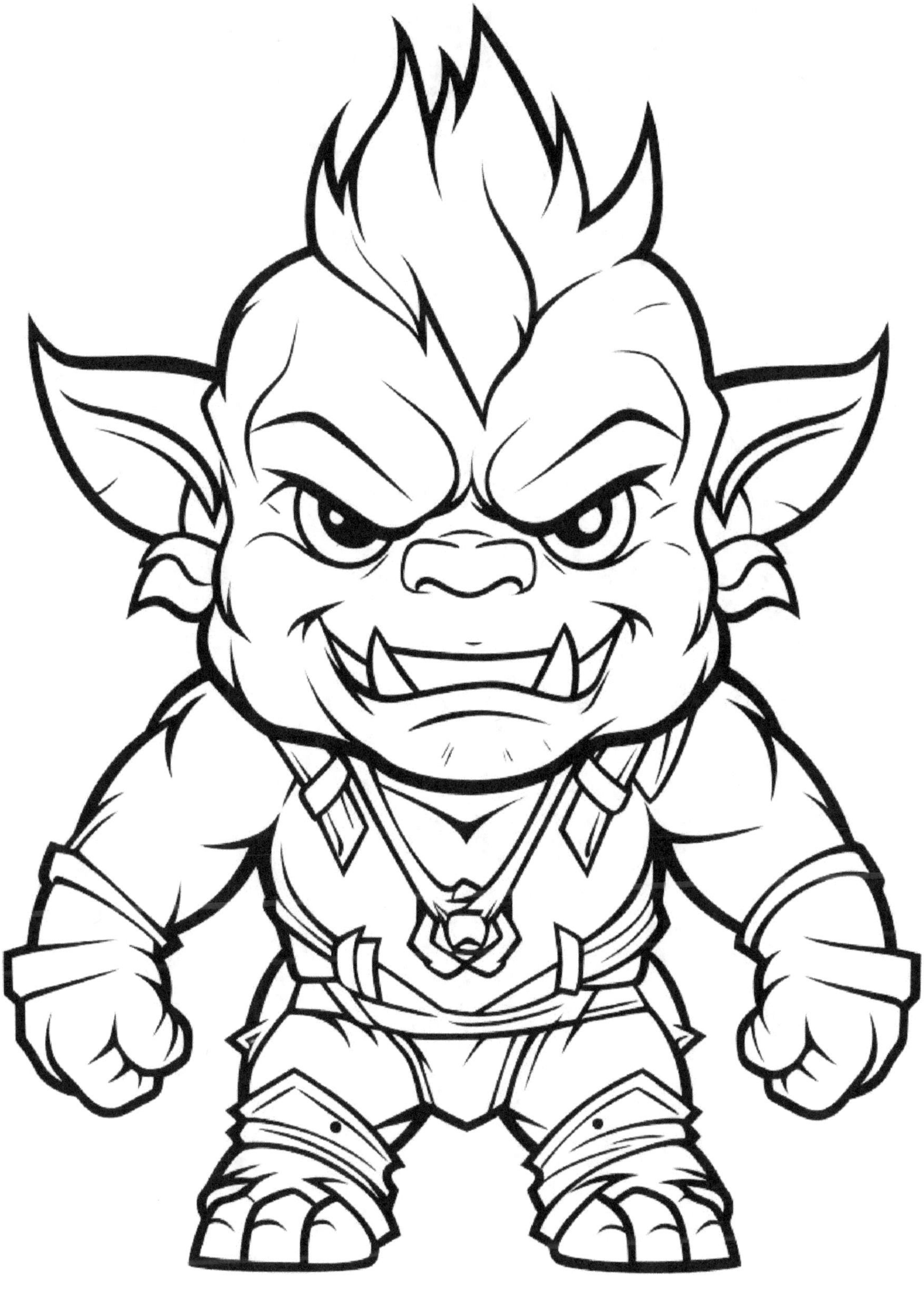

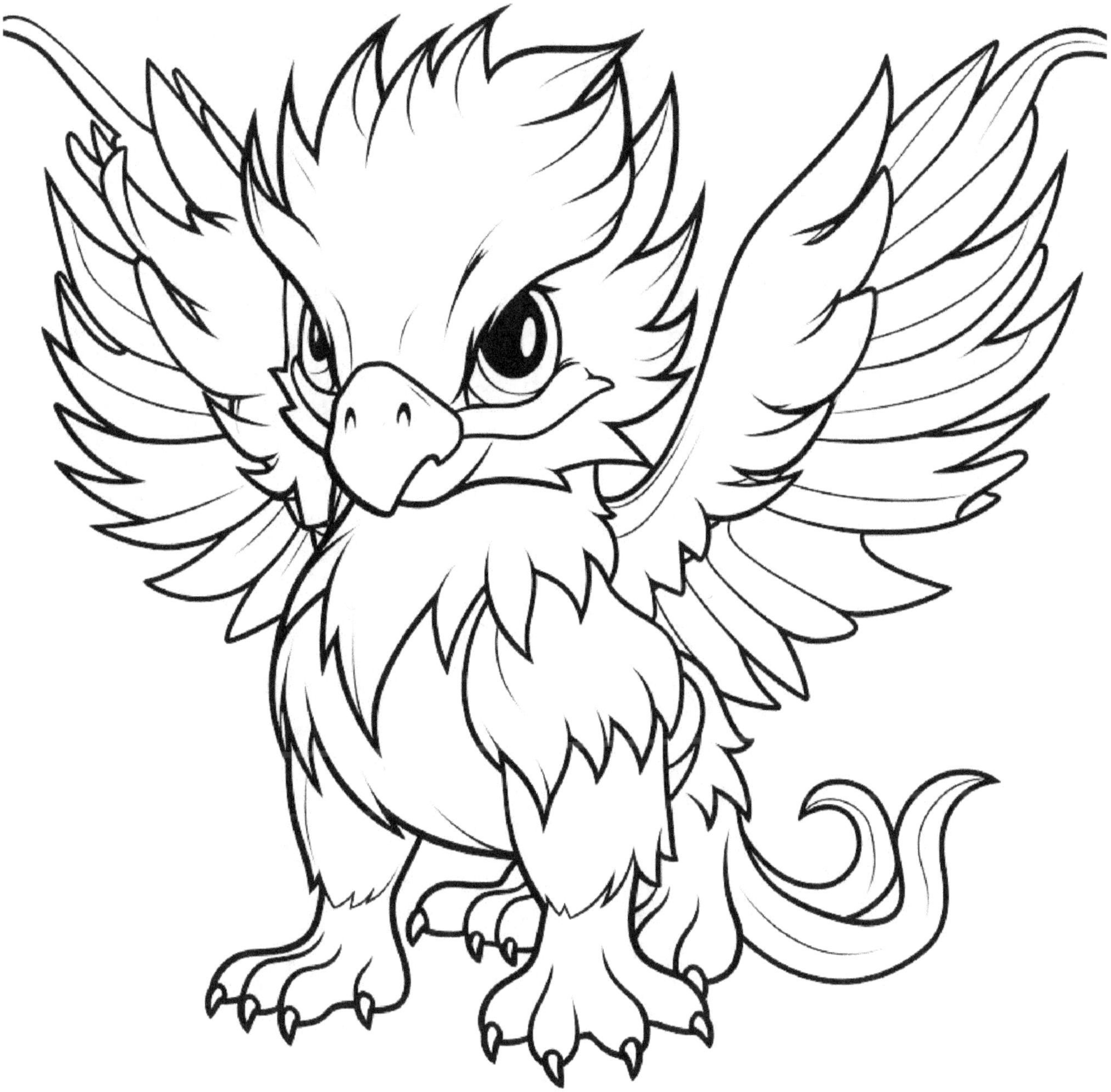

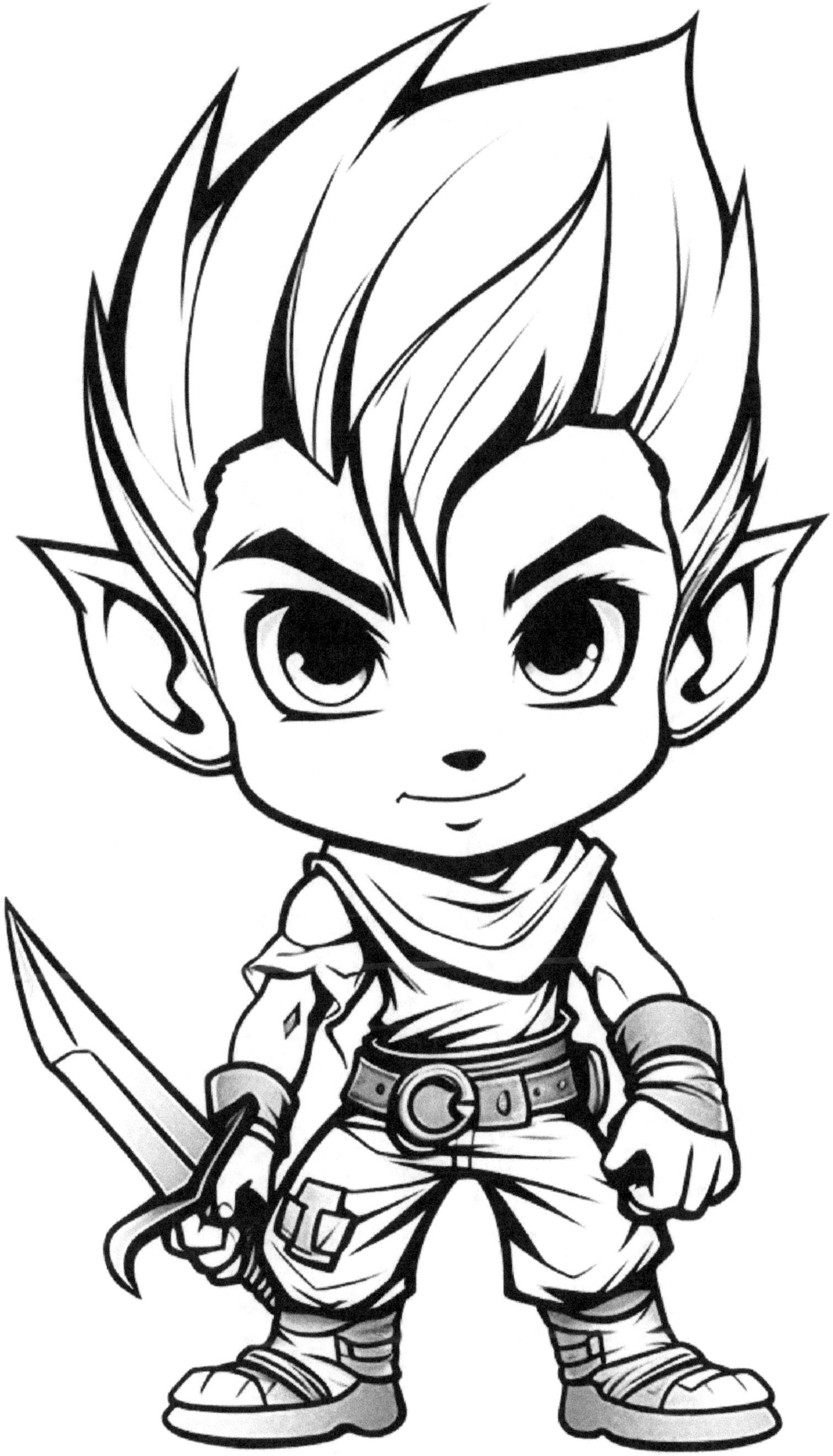

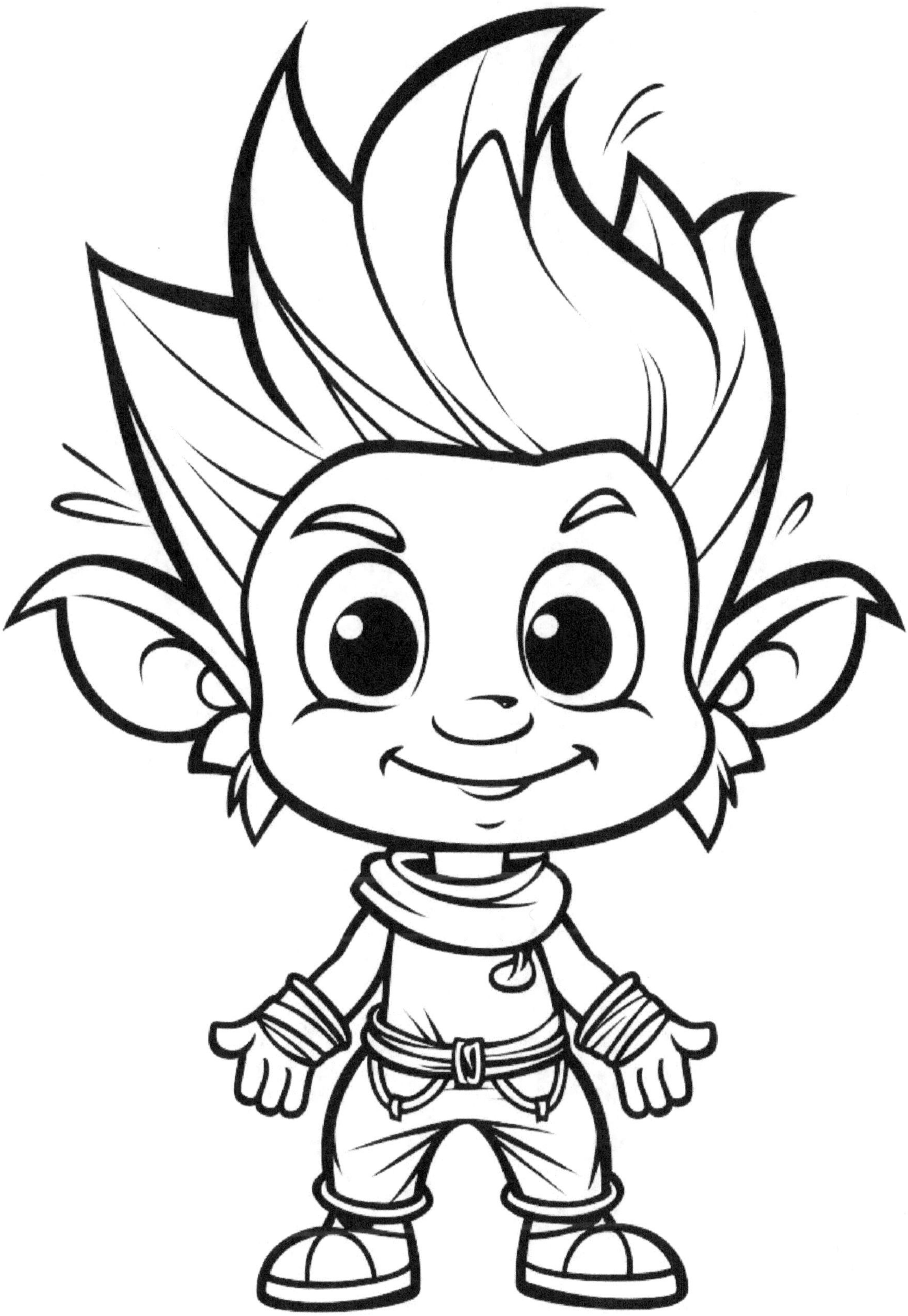

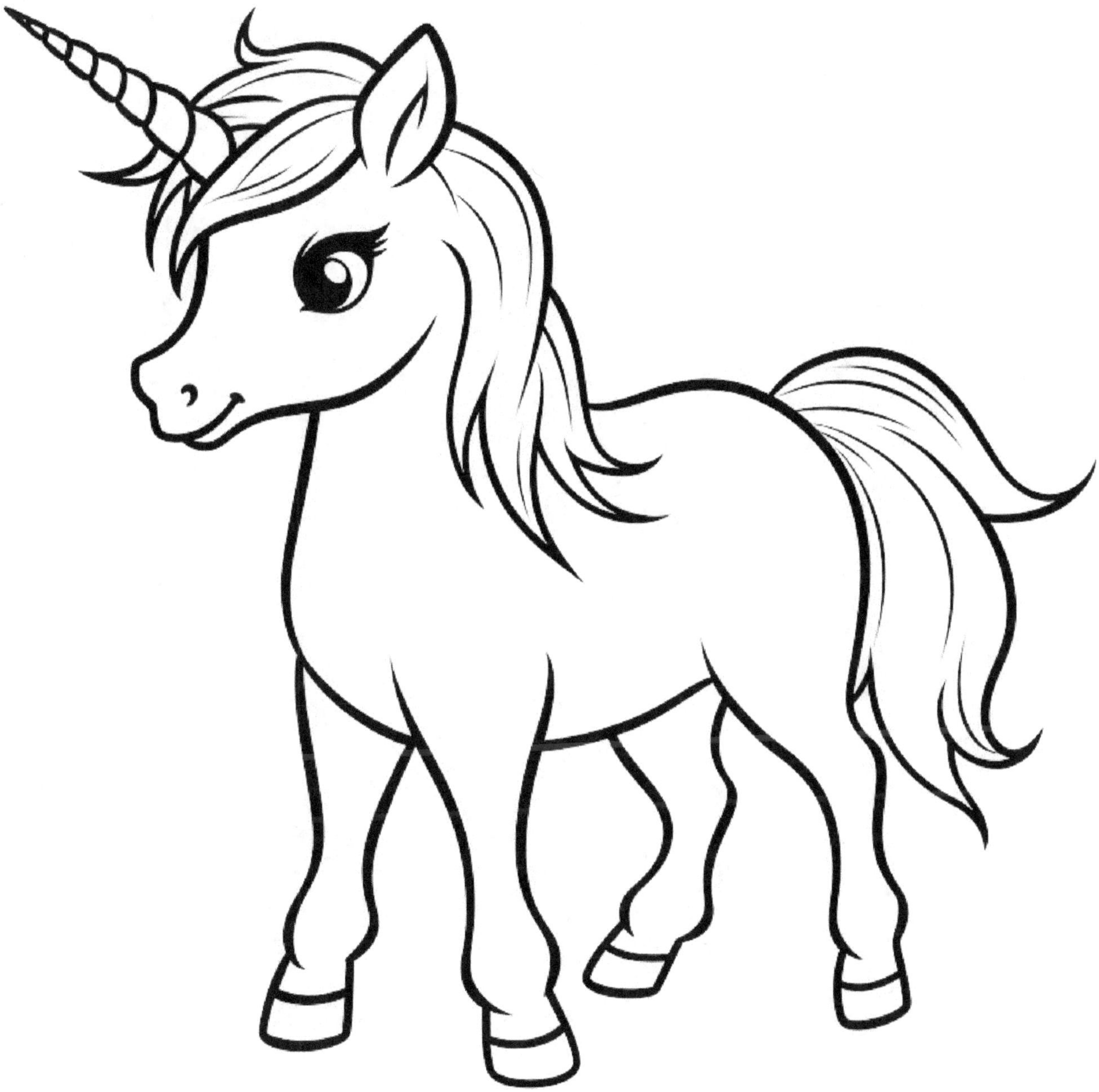

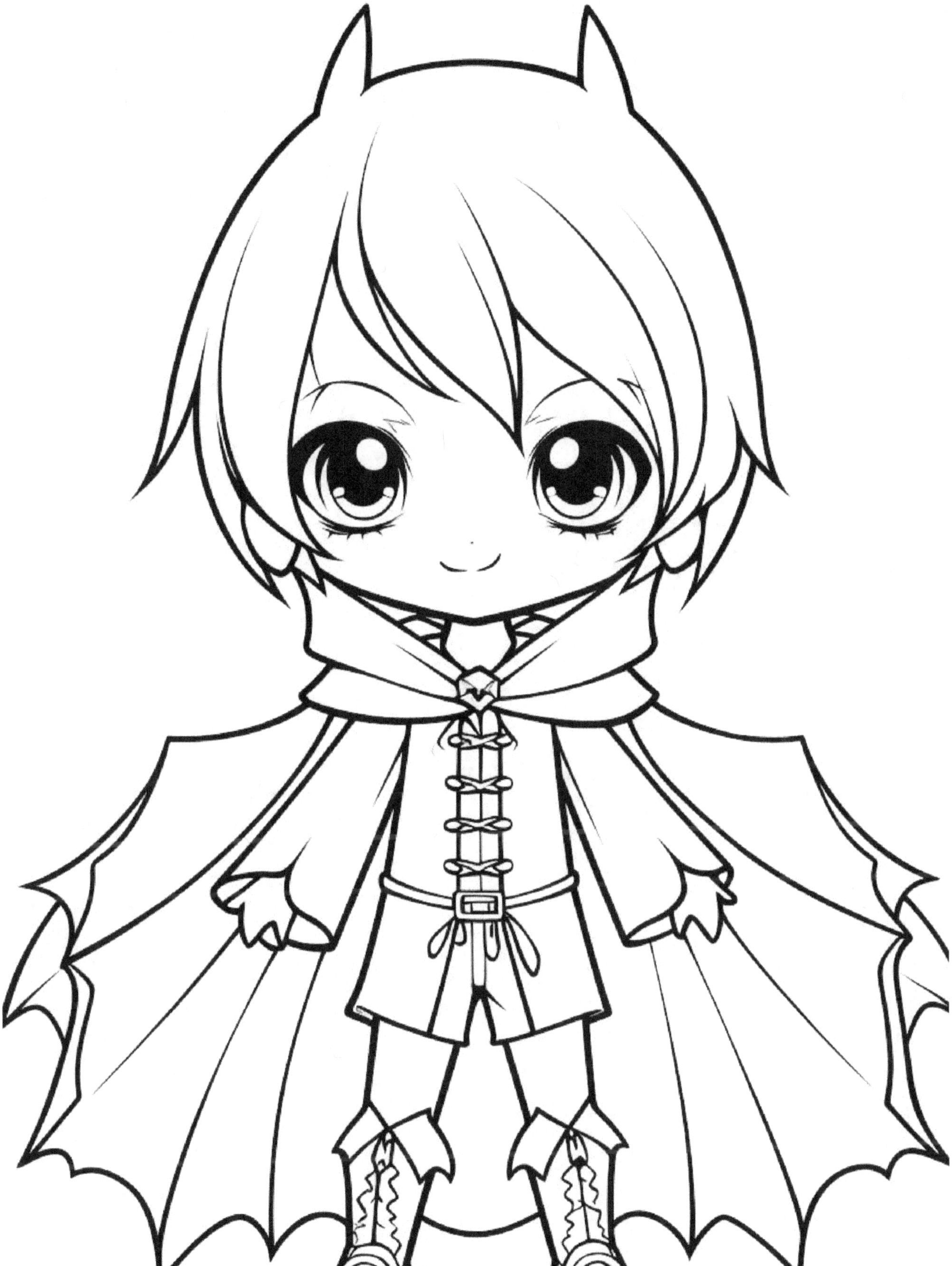

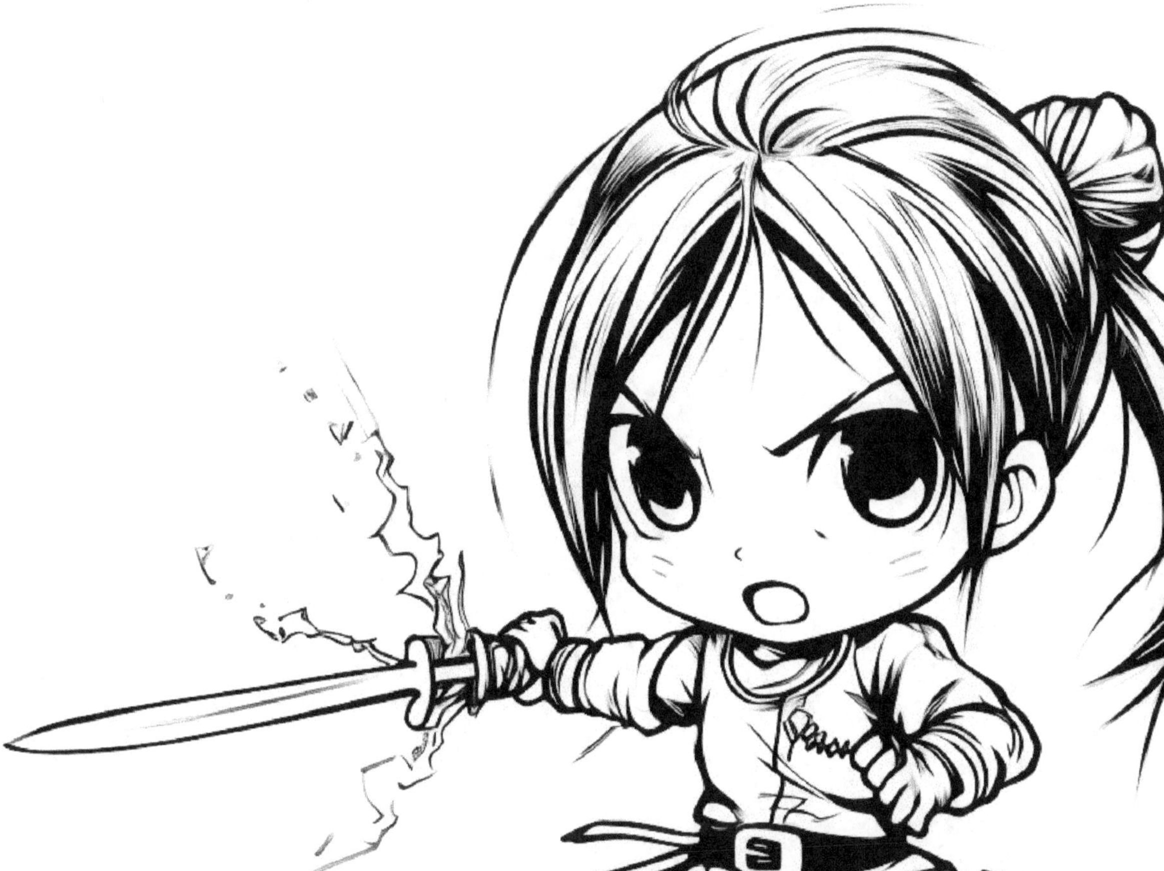

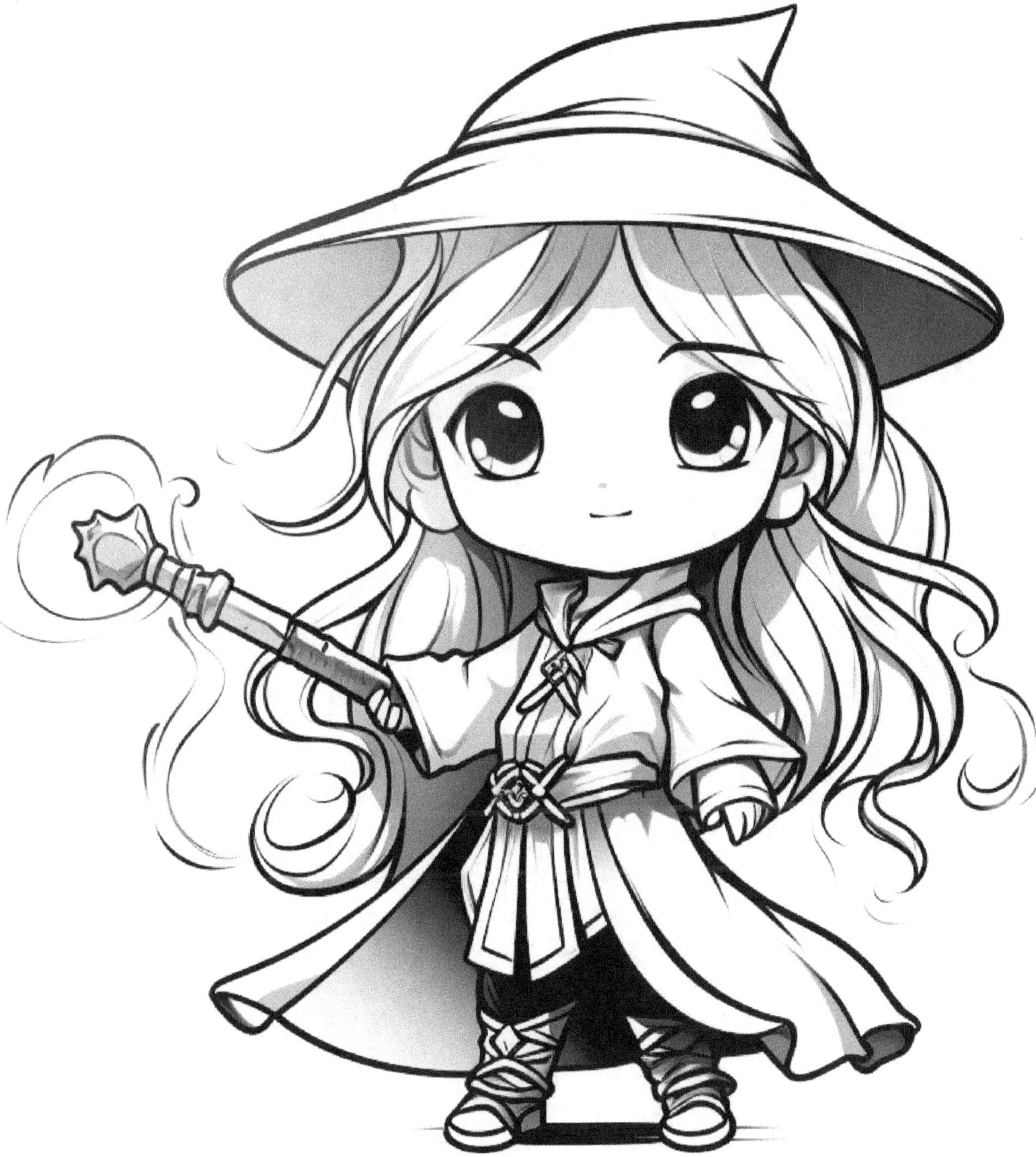

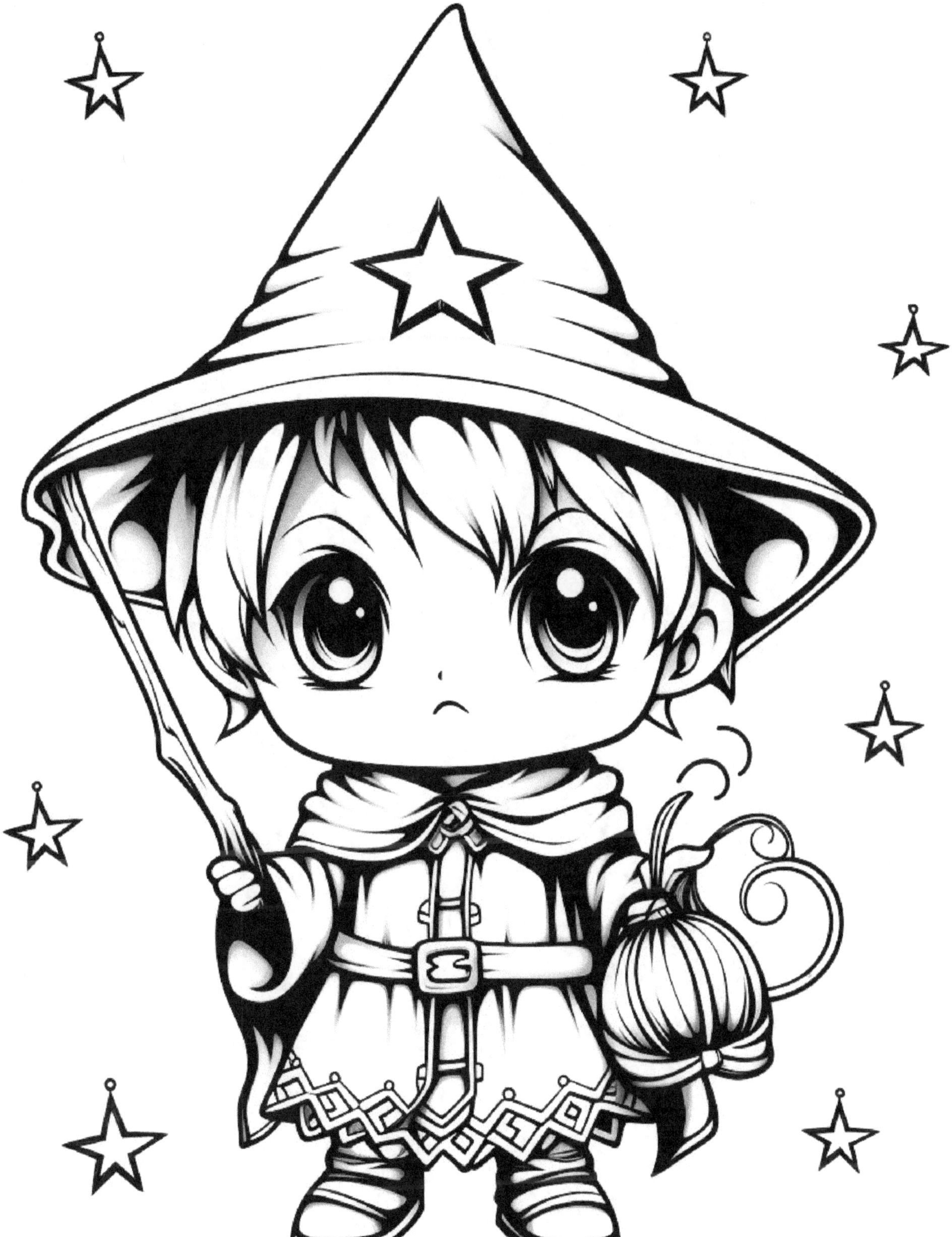

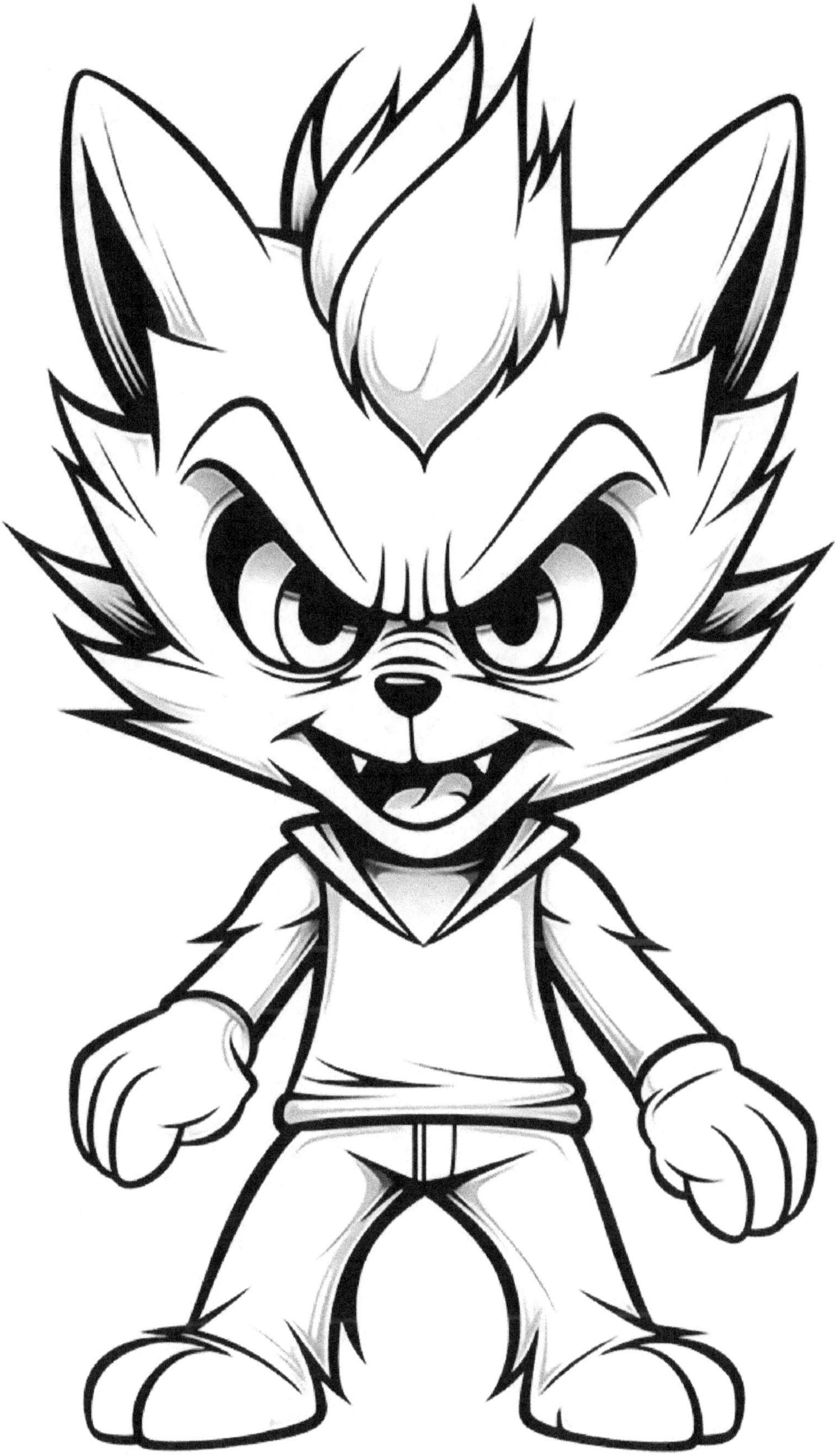

www.ingramcontent.com/pod-product-compliance
Lightning Source LLC
Chambersburg PA
CBHW082020230526
45466CB00022B/2887
9798397501637